BOOK

PREFACE

Many harmony textbooks provide difficult reading, with so many Do's & Dont's that learning harmony can be bewildering and off-putting.

The ABC of HARMONY attempts to offer a simple, concise approach. Basic requirements from primary to chromatic chords are covered as simply as possible.

BOOK A sets out to give the student a grasp of primary & secondary chords and their inversions, and experience in using standard chord progressions. The extensive exercises will help confidence and fluency.

To help to simplify matters, only single bass clef notes and two or three-part treble clef chords are used in the first 5 chapters. Essentials of part-writing are introduced in Chapter 6.

Harmony is about sound — only by playing the examples and exercises can a student begin to learn to hear and notice the results of what is written down. A purely mathematical approach is not musically satisfactory.

ROY WILKINSON
London 1991

BOOK

A

CONTENTS

CHAPTER 1

INTRODUCTION TO TRIADS, CHORDS & CADENCES

1.1 NAMES OF THE DEGREES OF THE SCALE

i.e. the names given to the notes of any scale, regardless of pitch or major / minor key.

Eg. 1.1(i)

Note of scale	Roman numeral	Name of degree
Key note	I	Tonic
2nd	II	Supertonic
3rd	III	Mediant
4th	IV	Subdominant
5th	V	Dominant
6th	VI	Submediant
7th	VII	Leading note (LN)

1.2 CHORDS AND TRIADS

a) These are a number of notes sounded together [three or more].

b) A **Triad** is the simplest form of chord - three notes.

c) It can be based on any degree of a major or minor scale.

d) A triad consists of: the root - i.e. the degree on which it is based.

the 3rd - major or minor, above the root.

the 5th - perfect, diminished or augmented, above the root.

e) Triads can be: major
minor } **Concordant**

diminished
augmented } **Discordant**

f)   **A major** triad   : consists of the root, major 3rd & perfect 5th
                                                   above the root.

g)   **A minor** triad   : the root, minor 3rd & perfect 5th
                                                   above the root.

h)   **A diminished** triad      : the root, minor 3rd & diminished 5th
                                                       above the root.

i)   **An augmented** triad      : the root, major 3rd & augmented 5th
                                                       above the root.

j)   Triads are described by the degree on which they are based, and are referred to by Roman
     numerals, as in Eg. 1.3(i) below.

     e.g. tonic triad (I), supertonic triad (II), etc.

k)   Melody notes are identified by Arabic numerals.

     e.g. tonic note (1), supertonic note (2), etc.

1.3   TRIADS IN A MAJOR KEY

Eg. 1.3(i)

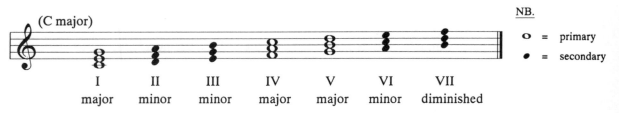

a)   **Primary triads** are those based on the   keynote or tonic (I),
                                                 subdominant   (IV),
                                                 dominant   (V)   of a scale

b)   **Secondary triads** are those on the other degrees of a scale.

c)   In a major scale,   the primary triads   I, IV & V   are major.
                            the secondary triads   II, III and VI   are minor,
                                                     VII   is diminished.

EXERCISE 1 — TRIADS OF MAJOR KEYS

1. Write the following triads **with key signatures**.
2. Aim for speed of response.

1) V of
F maj.

2) IV of
B♭ maj.

3) V of
F♯ maj.

4) IV of
A♭ maj.

5) V of
D♭ maj.

6) IV & V of
D maj.

7) IV & V of
B maj.

8) IV & V of
E maj.

9) IV & V of
E♭ maj.

10) IV & V of
G maj.

11) IV & V of
A maj.

12) II & VI of
D maj.

13) III & VI of
B maj.

14) II & V of
D♭ maj.

15) VI & IV of
A maj.

16) VI & V of
G maj.

17) IV & II of
A♭ maj.

18) VI & II of
E maj.

19) II & V of
F maj.

20) IV & VI of
E♭ maj.

21) VI, IV, V of
C maj.

22) VI, II, V of
F♯ maj.

23) VI, IV, II of
D maj.

24) I, VI, IV of
E maj.

25) II, IV, V of
A maj.

26) VI, II, V of
E♭ maj.

27) V, VI, III of
D♭ maj.

28) II, V, VII of
F♯ maj.

1.4   TRIADS IN A MINOR KEY

a)   The number of triads is greatly increased in minor keys because the submediant (6) and leading note (7) are different in the harmonic and melodic forms of the minor scale.

b)   The 6th and 7th degrees are raised by a semitone in an ascending melodic minor scale, but follow the key signature in a descending scale.

Eg. 1.4(i)

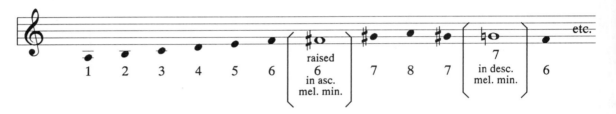

c)   This gives two choices for every minor key triad except I:

Eg. 1.4(ii)

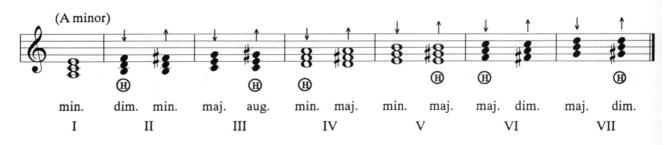

Ⓗ   identifies triads used in the harmonic minor scale.

↑   marks chords used in the **ascending** melodic minor.

↓   indicates chords used in a **descending** melodic minor.

d)   **Eg. 1.4(iii)**

NB.   *1.*   The **raised 6th and 7th** of A minor in bar 1 (F♯ & G♯).
                 They are harmonised by the **major** chords of IV and V,
                 [as shown by ↑ in Eg. 1.4(ii)]

         2.   In bar 2, the **lowered 6th and 7th** of A minor (F♮ & G♮)
                 are in a falling melody. They are harmonised by the **minor**
                 chords of V and IV.

         3.   The phrase ends on the dominant, which **must** be the
                 major V chord, so that A minor tonality (with G♯ as the LN)
                 is preserved.

EXERCISE 2 — TRIADS OF MINOR KEYS

1. Write the following triads with key signatures.
   (The **harmonic** form of the minor scale should be used.)

2. Aim for speed of response.

1)
IV of
D min.

2)
IV, V of
C min.

3)
V of
C♯ min.

4)
V of
B♭ min.

5)
V of
G min.

6)
V of
F min.

7)
IV, V of
E♭ min.

8)
IV, V of
E min.

9)
VI, V of
F♯ min.

10)
VI, IV of
A min.

11)
VI, IV of
B min.

12)
IV, V of
G♯ min.

13)
IV, V of
A min.

14)
VI, IV of
C♯ min.

15)
VI, IV of
B♭ min.

16)
VI of
E min.

17)
IV of
F♯ min.

18)
VI of
B min.

19)
IV, V of
D min.

20)
IV of
F min.

21)
VI of
E♭ min.

22)
VI, V of
C min.

23)
VI, V of
F min.

24)
VI, IV of
G min.

25)
VI, V of
B min.

26)
VI, IV of
D min.

27)
I, II of
B♭ min.

28)
III, II of
F♯ min.

EXERCISE 3 — MAJOR AND MINOR TRIADS

1. Complete the triads. Use accidentals.

The given note is the root, 3rd or 5th of a MAJOR triad.

The given note is the root, 3rd or 5th of a MINOR triad.

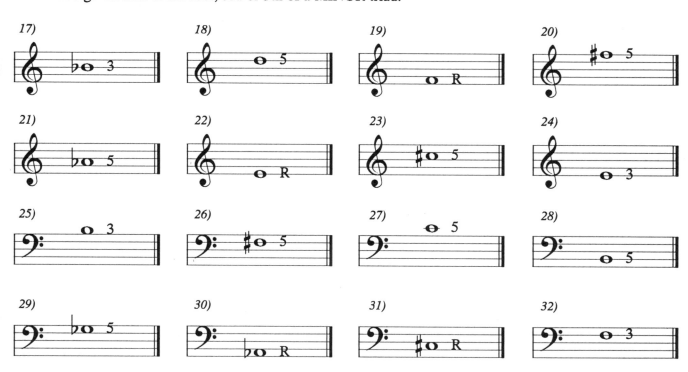

1.5 CHORDS

a)   When the three notes of a **triad** are increased by repeating one or more note at a different octave, the result is called a **chord**.

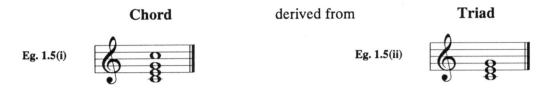

Eg. 1.5(i)   **Chord**   derived from   **Triad**   Eg. 1.5(ii)

b)   When writing a chord in 4 parts, the best note to double (repeat) is **usually** the root.

c)   Like triads, chords are described by the degree of the scale on which they are based.
      e.g.   tonic chord (I), submediant chord (VI), etc.

d)   Chords are described, also, by the name of the root of the chord.
      e.g.   The chord in Eg. 1.5(i) above is the chord of C major.

e)   **A common chord** is one which is major or minor.
      e.g.   In a major key, chords I to VI inclusive are common chords.
           In a minor key, the primary chords I, IV, V are common chords.

f)   In a minor key, the secondary chords may or may not be common chords. It will depend on whether the melodic or harmonic form of the scale is being used.
      e.g.   In Fig. 1.4(ii), II (harmonic) is diminished; however, II (melodic) is minor & therefore a common chord.

g)   VII, a diminished chord, is **not** a common chord.

h)   More elaborate chords will be covered later.

1.6 CHORD PROGRESSIONS

a)   Chords do not stand in isolation. They are related to each other within the traditional framework of tonality in Western music, and are used in progressions which are harmonically satisfying.

b)   The implied relationship of chords to each other within a major or minor tonality is reflected by referring to some chords as Primary and the others as Secondary. (Refer to §§1.3a, b, c).

1.7 CADENCES

a) Written music consists of phrases and sentences, built up into longer sections.

b) Certain chord progressions are used during or at the end of phrases, to indicate **points of rest**. In this, they are similar to punctuation marks.

c) They are called **cadences**. **Each** cadence consists of **two** chords.

d) There are **four** different forms of **cadence**:

Perfect,   Plagal,   Imperfect and **Interrupted.**

e) PERFECT CADENCE

V is followed by I at the end of a phrase.

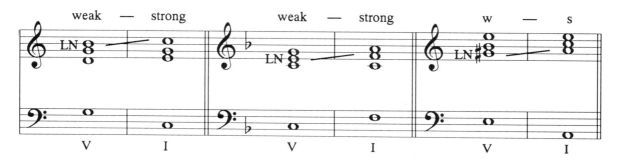

(i) It is a **strong final cadence**, the musical equivalent of a full stop.

(ii) The rhythm needs to be V (weak beat) to I (strong beat).

(iii) It is characterised by the rise of LN—1, and is at its strongest when the LN is the top note in V.

(iv) LN must rise a semitone to the root of I.

f) PLAGAL CADENCE

IV is followed by I at the end of a phrase.

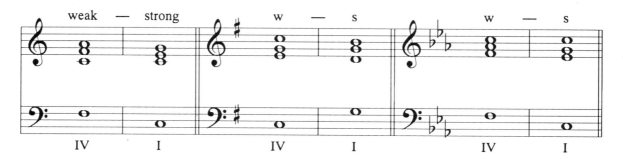

(i) It is another **strong final cadence** — a musical full-stop.

(ii) Rhythm again needs to be IV on a weak beat to I on a strong beat.

g)   IMPERFECT CADENCE

The first chord is usually I, IV, II or VI.

The second chord of the cadence **must** be V.

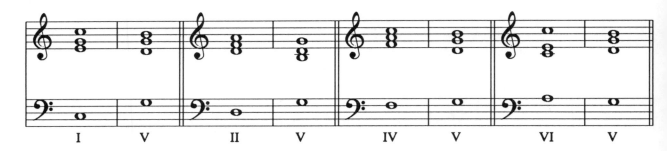

I   V   II   V   IV   V   VI   V

(i)   It is a **weaker** cadence than the Perfect or Plagal cadence.

(ii)   It is sometimes called a **half-close**.

(iii) Rhythm can be strong - weak, or weak - strong.

h)   INTERRUPTED CADENCE

V is followed by VI at the end of a phrase.

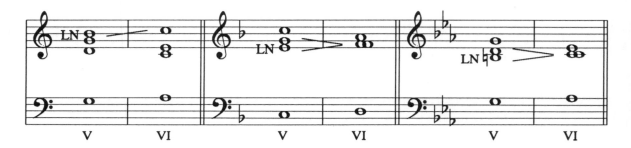

V   VI   V   VI   V   VI

(i)   It is **not** a strong cadence.

(ii)   Rhythm can be strong - weak, or weak - strong.

(iii) The 3rd of VI is usually doubled in this chord progression.

NB.   **Since the main concern of Chapters 1 – 5 is to make the student feel confident in the use of chord progressions, the only rules of part-writing which should be insisted on in these chapters are:**

   (i)   correct resolution of the LN wherever it occurs.

   (ii) avoidance in the outer parts of consecutive/parallel and hidden 5ths and 8ves. [Ref. pg.20]

   Certain rules about doubling need to be followed, also.

EXERCISE 4 — CADENCES

PERFECT CADENCES

1. Complete the following perfect cadences.

    NB.   1. Write 2 or 3 notes on the treble stave and 1 on the bass stave.
          2. Complete the bass or top part first, then add the remaining notes.
          3. Avoid moving the melody and bass parts in consecutive/hidden 5ths or 8ves.
          4. LN should rise. Indicate this with a line (see example).
          5. Do not double the major 3rd in I and V.
          6. When the melody moves 2 — 1 in this cadence, the LN rises and the 5th is omitted (see example).
          7. Indicate your chords with Roman numerals.

2.   Write perfect cadences in the keys of G, F, B♭, A♭ major, & F♯, B & C♯ minor.
     Write the bass part first.

PLAGAL CADENCES

1. Complete the following plagal cadences.

    NB.   1.   Add the bass part first, when it is omitted.
                 2.   Write 3 notes on the treble stave and 1 on the bass stave.
                 3.   Avoid moving the melody and bass parts in consecutive or hidden 5ths or 8ves.
                 4.   Avoid doubling the major 3rd in I and IV.
                 5.   Identify your chords with Roman numerals.

2.   Write plagal cadences in the keys of D♭, G♭ and F♯ major, and C♯, B and F♯ minor.
       Write the bass part first.

IMPERFECT CADENCES

1.   Write the following imperfect cadences.

NB.   1.   Add the bass part first, when it is omitted.
        2.   Write 3 notes on the treble stave and 1 on the bass stave.
        3.   Avoid moving the melody and bass parts in consecutive or hidden 5ths or 8ves.
        4.   Outer parts moving in opposite directions will give strength.
        5.   Remember the raised LN in minor keys. Move to it from a higher note (see example).
        6.   Double the 3rd of VI.
        7.   Indicate your chords with Roman numerals.

2.   Write various types of imperfect cadences in the keys of A, D♭ and B major, and E♭, C♯ and B minor.

INTERRUPTED CADENCES

1. Complete the following interrupted cadences.

NB. 1. Add the bass part first, when it is omitted.
2. Write 3 notes on the treble stave and 1 on the bass stave.
3. Avoid moving the melody and bass parts in consecutive or hidden 5ths or 8ves.
4. Outer parts moving in opposite directions will give strength.
5. However, V—VI is often written with the top part moving in 3rds with the bass. In that case, the other notes **must** move downwards, with the 3rd of VI doubled. Study the example.
6. Remember that the LN rises in V—VI; mark it with a line.
7. Indicate your chords with Roman numerals.

2.   Write interrupted cadences in the keys of F♯, E and B♭ major, and C, G♯ and B♭ minor.

CHAPTER 2

PRIMARY CHORDS IN ROOT POSITION & 1ST INVERSION

2.1 THE USE OF PRIMARY CHORDS IN ROOT POSITION

a) 'Root position' describes the arrangement of the notes of a chord or triad when the lowest (or bass) note is also the root of the chord. The 3rd and 5th of the chord will also lie above it.

e.g. is the chord of C major in root position.

b) Because the notes are arranged with the 3rd and 5th above the bass, it is referred to as a $\frac{5}{3}$ chord. (See Chapter 4 - Figured Bass).

c) The primary chords (I, IV, V) always give strong satisfactory chord progressions.

   I—V,   I—IV,   V—I,   IV—I,   IV—V,

   I—IV—V,   IV—V—I,   IV—I—V,

   I—IV—I—V,   I—IV—V—I,   V—I—IV—V—I

   etc.

d) From this, it can be seen that chords with roots a perfect 4th or 5th apart will always sound good.

e) V—IV is less satisfactory.

f) Root position chords are usually identified by the letter "a" after the Roman numerals. e.g. Ia, IIa, etc.

2.2   POINTS TO BE OBSERVED WHEN WORKING FUTURE EXERCISES

a)   (i)   Decide on the key, then on the cadence(s).

   (ii)   Decide on the approach chord(s) to the cadence(s).

   (iii) Look for standard progressions, starting at the beginning of the phrase.

   (iv) Complete the other outer part.

   (v)   Fill in the harmonies.

b)   Outer parts moving in opposite directions will give strength and will help to avoid errors.

c)   Avoid moving in 5ths or 8ves in the same direction (called "consecutive or parallel 5ths/8ves") :

Eg. 2.2(i)   Eg. 2.2(ii)

d)   Avoid "hidden" (sometimes called "exposed") 5ths/8ves. These occur when the outer voices move in the same direction on to a perfect 5th or 8ve, with the top part not moving by step.

Eg. 2.2(iii)

e)   A rising augmented interval should not be written.

Eg. 2.2(iv)

Aug. 5th

This can be avoided by moving to the "faulty" note from above:

Eg. 2.2(v)

Dim. 4th

f)   Chords whose roots are a perfect 5th or 4th apart will always sound good.

g)   A chord repeated strong-weak is good. The bass will usually move from the root position to the 1st inversion or vice versa.

h)   A chord or bass-note repeated weak-strong within a phrase is poor and must be avoided. A particular case of this is the repetition of a chord across a barline.

i)   Aim for smooth movement, using "common notes" as much as possible. The bass will often move more boldly than the other parts.

j)   When one outer part moves by leap, it is better to try to keep the other still or to move it in contrary motion.

k)   Remember :   LN rises a semitone in V—I.

LN in a minor tonality must be raised.

EXERCISE 5 — PRIMARY CHORDS IN ROOT POSITION

1. Write the following primary chord progressions in the major and minor keys of 0 to 4 ♯s and ♭s key signatures.

   a) I—V   b) I—IV   c) V—I   d) IV—I   e) IV—V

   f) I—IV—V   g) IV—V—I   h) IV—I—V   i) I—IV—I—V

NB.   1.   Write 2 or 3 notes in the treble stave and 1 in the bass stave.

2.   Complete the following. Write 3 notes on the treble stave and 1 on the bass stave.

NB.   1.   Use Roman numerals to indicate the chords used (see example).
         2.   Add the bass part first, when it is omitted.
         3.   Remember the raised LN in minor keys.
         4.   Indicate LN—tonic.

1) *Example:*   C major

IV   V   I

2.3   THE FIRST INVERSION OF PRIMARY CHORDS

a)   A chord or triad is described as an **inversion** when its lowest note is **not** the root of the chord.

b)   A chord or triad is in its **first inversion** when the **lowest note is the 3rd** above the root.

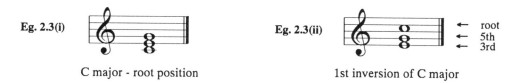

C major - root position   1st inversion of C major

c)   In this inversion, the chord is arranged with intervals of a 6th and a 3rd above the bass note.

For this reason it is called a $\frac{6}{3}$ chord, or more often just a "6th chord" —
or "chord of the 6th". (Refer to Chapter 4 - Figured Bass)

d)   A first inversion chord is usually identified by the use of the letter "b" after the Roman numeral.
      e.g.   Example 2.3(ii) above is Ib in the key of C major.

e)   The 1st inversion triads of C major look like this:

Eg. 2.3(iv)

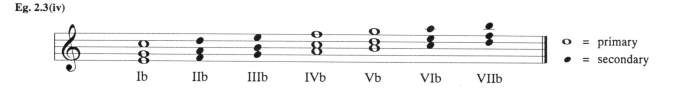

Ib   IIb   IIIb   IVb   Vb   VIb   VIIb

O = primary
• = secondary

f)   **Do not** double the bass-note of a 1st inversion **major** chord.

g)   The 1st inversion triads of A minor look like this:

Eg. 2.3(v)

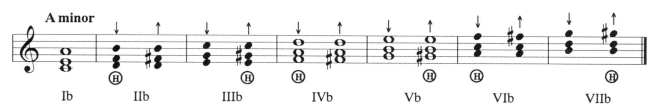

Ib   IIb   IIIb   IVb   Vb   VIb   VIIb

Again, the harmonic/melodic minor scales give alternative chords.

The choice of chord depends on whether ascending or descending movement is involved.

[Compare this with Eg. 1.4(ii)]

EXERCISE 6 — 1ST INVERSION PRIMARY TRIADS

1. Write the following 1st inversion triads. Insert the correct key signature.
2. Use the harmonic form of the minor keys.

MAJOR

1) *Example:*
Ib in
G maj.

2)
IVb in
B maj.

3)
IVb in
D maj.

4)
Ib in
A♭ maj.

5)
IVb in
G maj.

6)
Ib in
E♭ maj.

7)
Ib in
B♭ maj.

8)
IVb in
C maj.

9)
Vb in
C maj.

10)
Vb in
A maj.

11)
Vb in
F♯ maj.

12)
Vb in
D♭ maj.

MINOR

13)
Ib in
F min.

14)
Ib in
C♯ min.

15)
IVb in
C♯ min.

16)
Vb in
C min.

17)
Vb in
B♭ min.

18)
IVb in
F♯ min.

19)
Vb in
B min.

20)
IVb in
A min.

21)
Vb in
G min.

22)
Ib in
B min.

23)
Ib in
F♯ min.

24)
Vb in
D min.

2.4   USE OF FIRST INVERSIONS OF THE PRIMARY CHORDS

a)   First inversions mixed with root position chords give a smoother and more interesting result than when only root position chords are used.

b)   Compare Eg. 2.4(i) with Eg. 2.4 (ii). In the second of these, the 1st inversion chords lighten the harmonic result:

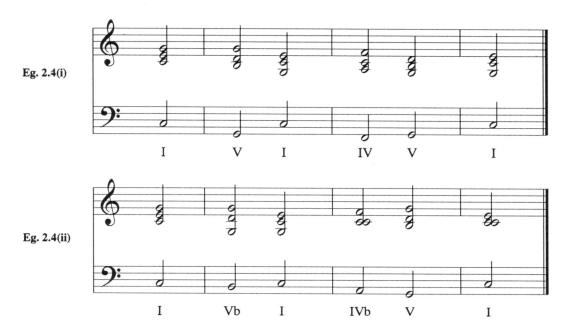

c)   The use of 1st inversions for the first chord of the various imperfect cadence progressions gives four extra forms of this cadence:

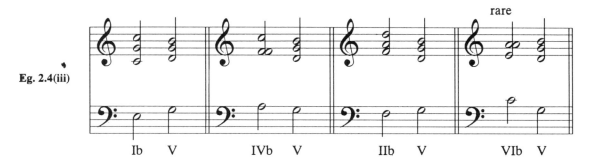

Of these, Ib and IVb (primary chords) are commonly used.

IIb (secondary chord) — V is probably the commonest of all.

VIb (secondary chord) — V is rarely used.

d)   Use of 1st inversion chords should be guided by the smooth movement of the outer parts. The smoother the movement of one or both of the outer parts, the more satisfactory the result will be.

e)   The bass of a **major** $\frac{6}{3}$ chord must **not** be doubled.

It is common for the bass of a **minor** $\frac{6}{3}$ chord to be doubled, however.

EXERCISE 7 — 1ST INVERSIONS OF PRIMARY CHORDS

1.   Add chords to the following bass parts. Use 1st inversions as indicated (by b).

NB.   1.   Write 2 notes on the treble stave and 1 on the bass stave.
       2.   Use Roman numerals to identify your chords.
       3.   Remember that the LN rises in V—I.

2.   Add notes below the given melodies, using a mixture of root position and 1st inversion chords.

   NB.   1.   Write one note only on the bass stave.
          2.   Indicate the chords you choose.
          3.   Use a 1st inversion chord where b is printed.

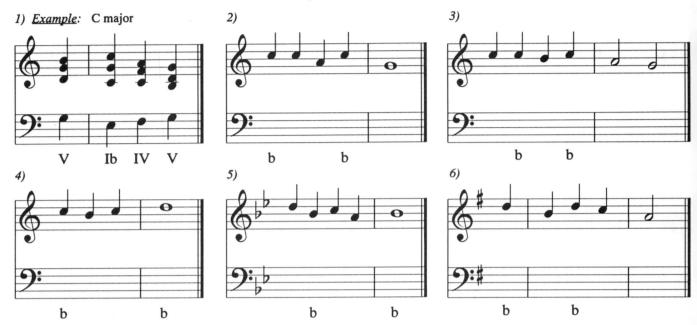

3.   Introduce 1st inversions in suitable places in the following exercises. Indicate your choice.

   NB.   1.   Complete the bass part first.

4.   Add chords to the following bass parts. Choice of chords (root & 1st inversion) is yours.

NB.   1.   Add 3 notes on the treble stave.
       2.   Indicate your chords and inversions.
       3.   Remember the rising LN in V—I.

CHAPTER 3

PRIMARY CHORDS IN 2ND INVERSION

3.1 SECOND INVERSIONS OF CHORDS

a)   A chord is in its **second inversion** when its **lowest note is the 5th** above the root:

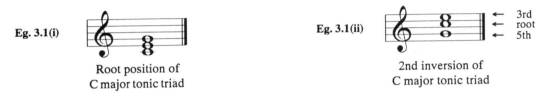

Eg. 3.1(i)   Root position of C major tonic triad

Eg. 3.1(ii)   2nd inversion of C major tonic triad   ← 3rd / ← root / ← 5th

b)   In this position, there are intervals of a 4th and a 6th above the bass:

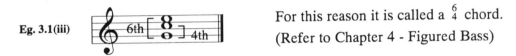

Eg. 3.1(iii)   6th ⎡ ⎤ 4th

For this reason it is called a $^6_4$ chord.
(Refer to Chapter 4 - Figured Bass)

c)   A second inversion chord is usually identified by the letter "c" following the Roman numeral. Eg. 3.1 (ii) above is Ic in the key of C major.

d)   Second inversion triads of C major look like this:

Eg. 3.1(iv)

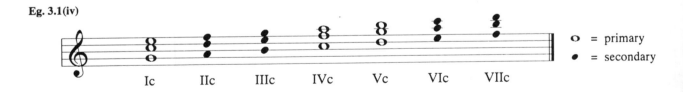

Ic   IIc   IIIc   IVc   Vc   VIc   VIIc

o = primary
• = secondary

e)   A second inversion chord can **not** be used unless it is

    i)   part of a cadence   cadential $^6_4$ chord.

            .....hence the names.....

    ii)   in a passing progression   passing $^6_4$ chord.

f)   Only Ic, Vc and IVc are used.

g)   The **best** note to double in any 4-part 2nd inversion chord is its **bass-note**.

3.2   CADENTIAL 2ND INVERSION

a)   **Only two chords are used** as cadential $\frac{6}{4}$ s — Ic (frequently)   and   IVc (occasionally).

b)   Always the cadential $\frac{6}{4}$ chord is followed by a root position chord **with the same bass-note**:

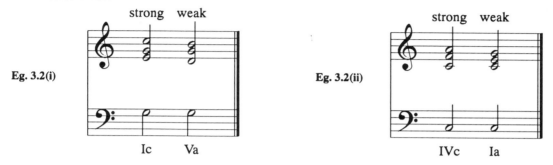

Eg. 3.2(i)   Ic   Va   Eg. 3.2(ii)   IVc   Ia

c)   As its name indicates, this chord progression is associated with a cadence, and it is frequently used.

d)   The **6th** above the bass of the $\frac{6}{4}$ chord moves to the **5th** of the next chord.

        The **4th** above the bass of the $\frac{6}{4}$ chord moves to the **3rd** of the next chord.

        The **bass-note** of each chord is doubled.

e)   It can be used as the 1st chord of an imperfect cadence:

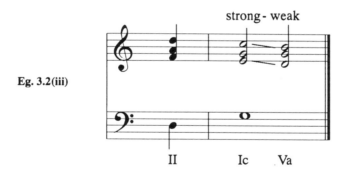

Eg. 3.2(iii)   II   Ic   Va

        NB: the part-writing, which needs to be strictly observed.

f)   It can also be used to precede a perfect cadence:

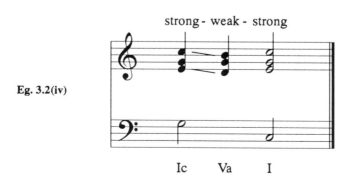

Eg. 3.2(iv)   Ic   Va   I

g)   It can also be used to precede an interrupted cadence:

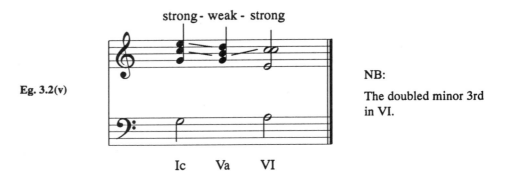

Eg. 3.2(v)

NB:

The doubled minor 3rd
in VI.

h)   The Ic chord must **always** be on a stronger beat than Va.

i)   It is not satisfactory for Ic to be preceded by a 1st inversion of a different chord, **unless**
the bass is approached by step.

Eg. 3.2(vi)

j)   IVc is sometimes used, though comparatively rarely.

It acts as a decorated form of perfect or plagal cadence:

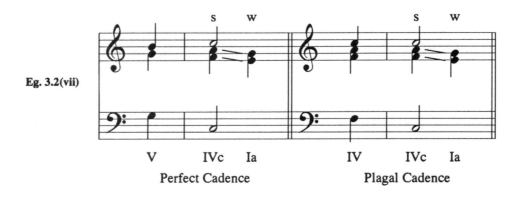

Eg. 3.2(vii)

EXERCISE 8 — CADENTIAL 2ND INVERSION CHORDS

1.   Complete the following using cadential 2nd inversions on each 1st chord.

NB.   1.   Use 2 or 3 notes in the treble stave.
      2.   Indicate the chords used.
      3.   Move the 6th to the 5th, and
             the 4th to the 3rd; and add the doubled note.
      4.   Remember that the LN must rise in V—I; mark the LN—tonic movement.
      5.   VARY THE NOTE ARRANGEMENT.

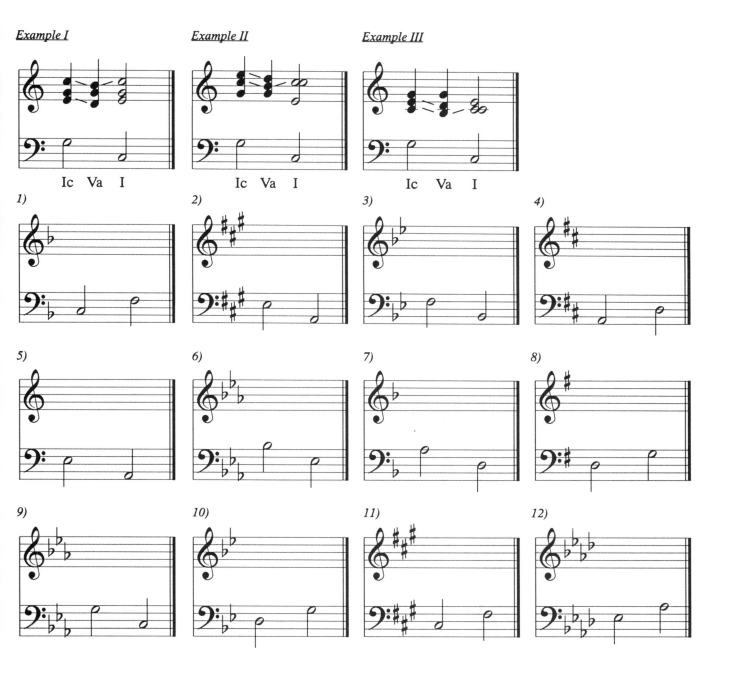

3.3   THE PASSING 2ND INVERSION

a)   **Only Ic or Vc** can be used as a **passing** $\frac{6}{4}$

b)   This progression is one that is often used.

c)   It is most easily identified when an outer part moves 3–2–1 or 1–2–3:

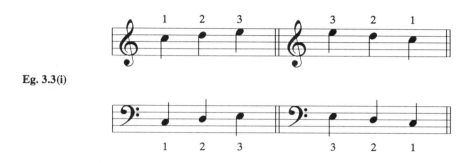

Eg. 3.3(i)

d)   When this happens, the other outer part uses the same 3 notes in contrary motion:

Eg. 3.3(ii)

e)   The chords are completed as follows:

        one middle voice moves 8–7–8;   the 4th voice moves 5–5–5.

Eg. 3.3(iii)

f)   Unlike the cadential $\frac{6}{4}$, the passing $\frac{6}{4}$ can occur on either a strong or a weak beat.

g)   Sometimes, this progression is used for notes 4–5–6 / 6–5–4.

In that case, the movement of notes in IVb—Ic—IVa (or IVa—Ic—IVb) is similar.

Eg. 3.3(iv)

EXERCISE 9 — PASSING 2ND INVERSION CHORDS

1. Complete the following using passing 2nd inversions (Ia—Vc—Ib and IVa—Ic—IVb).

NB.
1. Use 3 notes in the treble stave.
2. Indicate your choice of chords.
3. Add the other outer part to the given part.
4. Complete the harmonies.

MINOR KEYS

NB.   the raised LN.

EXERCISE 10 — INCORPORATING PRIMARY CHORDS AND CADENCES

1.   Complete the following.

NB.   1.   Add 3 parts on the treble stave.
      2.   Use inversions where suitable, looking out for cadential and passing chords.
      3.   Decide 1st on the key and cadence, and then the approach chord to the cadence.
      4.   Avoid parallel 5ths and 8ves between parts (the interrupted cadence needs special care).
      5.   **Some** hints are given — b denotes a 1st inversion chord, c denotes a 2nd inversion chord.

CHAPTER 4

FIGURED BASSES

a) This is a shorthand notation of harmony.

b) Figures are placed beneath a written bass-note to indicate the chord to be used.

c) The figures represent the intervals above the given note.

d) $\begin{smallmatrix}5\\3\end{smallmatrix}$ beneath a note requires the **diatonic** 3rd and 5th to be played. [diatonic: notes belonging to the key.]

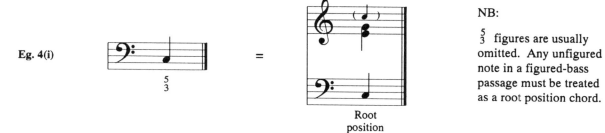

Eg. 4(i)

Root position

NB:

$\begin{smallmatrix}5\\3\end{smallmatrix}$ figures are usually omitted. Any unfigured note in a figured-bass passage must be treated as a root position chord.

e) 6 stands for $\begin{smallmatrix}6\\3\end{smallmatrix}$. This requires the 3rd and 6th above the given bass, i.e. a 1st inversion chord.

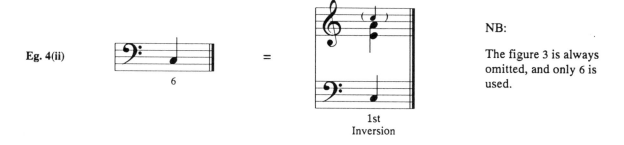

Eg. 4(ii)

1st Inversion

NB:

The figure 3 is always omitted, and only 6 is used.

f) $\begin{smallmatrix}6\\4\end{smallmatrix}$ requires the 4th and 6th above the given bass, i.e. a 2nd inversion chord.

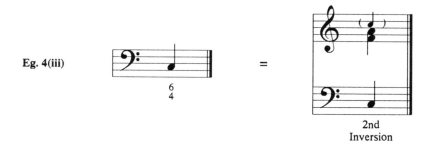

Eg. 4(iii)

2nd Inversion

g) If one of the added notes is not part of the key, the chromatic alteration is indicated by placing ♯ , ♭ , or ♮ before or after the relevant figure.

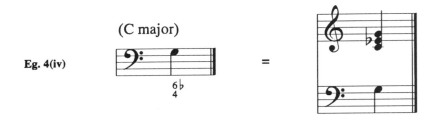

Here, the E♭ required in the $\frac{6}{4}$ chord is shown in the figured bass.

h) If the chord 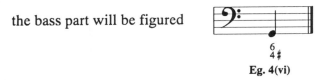 in the key of C is needed,

the bass part will be figured

i)   Eg. 4(vii)

j) An accidental without a figure refers to the 3rd of the $\frac{5}{3}$ chord.

k) An accidental below the figure 6 alone implies a $\frac{6}{3}$ (1st inversion) chord with the 3rd altered.

Eg. 4(ix)

l) The cadential 2nd inversion chords are usually referred to as $\frac{6}{4}$ $\frac{5}{3}$ chords (which clearly shows the movement of each part).

m) Figuring of more elaborate chords will be dealt with later.

EXERCISE 11 — FIGURED BASSES

1. Write suitable chords above the figured basses:

NB.   Add 2 notes only, on the treble stave.

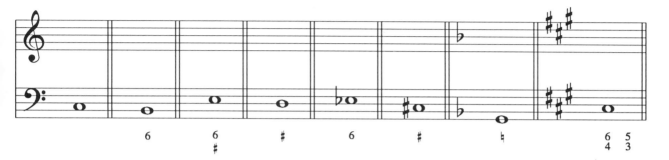

2. Complete the following.

NB.   1. Use 3 notes on the treble stave.
        2. Try to have smoothness in the added parts, avoiding wide leaps.
        3. Remember the raised LN in minor keys. It is not always figured.

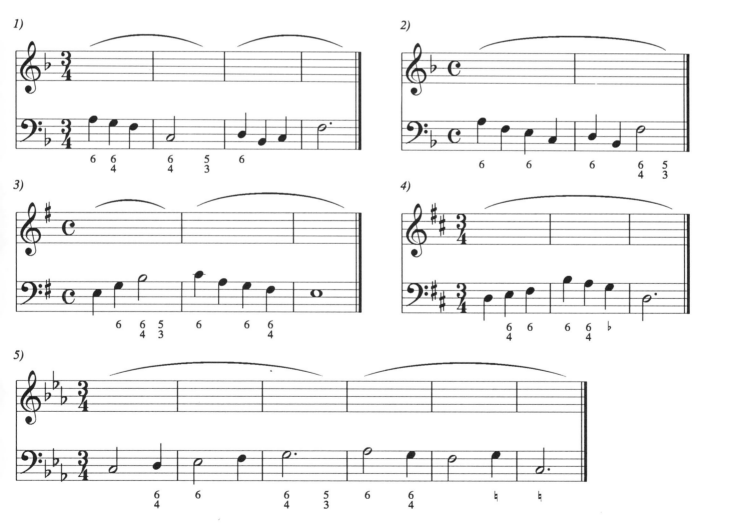

CHAPTER 5

SECONDARY CHORDS

5.1 SECONDARY CHORDS

a)   Secondary chords are II, III, VI and VII. The most frequently used are II and VI.

b)   When using both primary and secondary chords, remember that chords whose roots fall in 3rds will always sound good.
Roots rising in 3rds are generally less effective. (I — III is an exception).

5.2 THE SUPERTONIC CHORD (II)

a)   It is very frequently used before V.

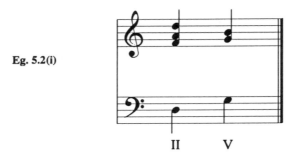

Eg. 5.2(i)

II   V

b)   This makes it a strong approach chord to the perfect cadence.
IIb is its usual position in this progression, giving a smoother bass-line.

Eg. 5.2(ii)

IIb   V   I

NB: The bass of IIb should normally be doubled.

c)   Since it is a general rule that chords with roots a perfect 4th or 5th apart will give a strong progression, VI—IIb or VI—II are very effective:-

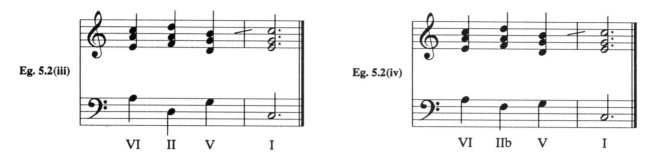

Eg. 5.2(iii)   VI II V   I   Eg. 5.2(iv)   VI IIb V   I

d)   IV—II is good also because the roots fall a 3rd.

Eg. 5.2(v)   IV II V   VI

e)   I—II—V is good, though I—IIb—V is even better:

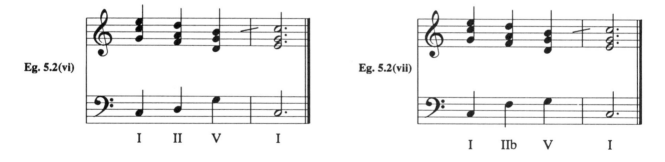

Eg. 5.2(vi)   I II V   I   Eg. 5.2(vii)   I IIb V   I

f)   II—I, II—III and III—II are little used.

g)   <u>MINOR KEY</u>

        In a minor key, IIa is diminished; therefore IIb is more common.

Eg. 5.2(viii)   NB:

                                         The bass of the chord should be doubled.

                              IIb V   I

EXERCISE 12 — THE SUPERTONIC CHORD

NB. 1. Write 3 notes in the treble stave and 1 in the bass stave.
2. Indicate the chords used.

13)

14)

VI

15)

IIb

16)

IIb

5.3 THE SUBMEDIANT CHORD (VI)

a) A very important chord, which has already been introduced in §§1.7 on Cadences.

VI—V is an imperfect cadence progression.

V—VI is an interrupted cadence.

b) I—VI is a strong progression, often used. It is a good way of harmonising the tonic note repeated strong / weak (see below).

c) VI—IV is another often-used progression, based (like I—VI) on roots falling in 3rds, eg. I—VI—IV—I.

Eg. 5.3(i)

I   VI   IV   I

d) VI—II is a very good progression, referred to in §§5.2c.

e) VI—III and III—VI are effective, their roots being a perfect interval apart.

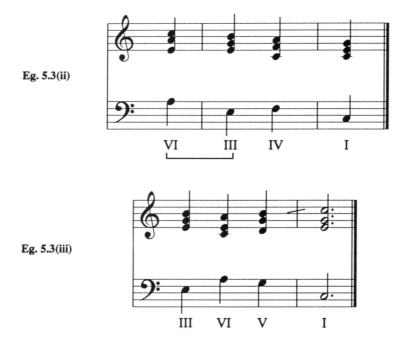

Eg. 5.3(ii)

VI   III   IV   I

Eg. 5.3(iii)

III   VI   V   I

f)   VI is more often found in root position than in 1st inversion. The best note to double is the 3rd of the chord.

g)   <u>MINOR KEY</u>

In a minor key, VI is a major chord (when based on the lowered 6th).

Eg. 5.3(iv)

VI in C minor

h)   In VI—V or V—VI in the minor form, the 3rd of chord VI **should** be doubled.

Eg. 5.3(v)

I   VI   V

EXERCISE 13 — THE SUBMEDIANT CHORD

NB.   1.   Write 3 notes in the treble stave and 1 in the bass stave.
            2.   Indicate the chords used.

5.4   THE MEDIANT CHORD (III)

a)   It is less frequently used than II or VI, and quite restricted.

b)   Standard progressions including III are:

i)   VI—III—IV—I / V, when the melody moves 8–7–6–5.

Eg. 5.4(i)

ii)   I—III—IV—V is an alternative for an 8–7–6–5 melody.

Eg. 5.4(ii)

c)   III—VI is strong (roots a perfect interval apart), and gives an alternative harmonisation when the melody moves 7–8.

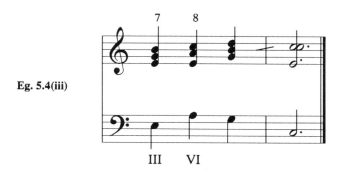

Eg. 5.4(iii)

d)   (i)   V—III—VI or V—IIIb—VI give good results.

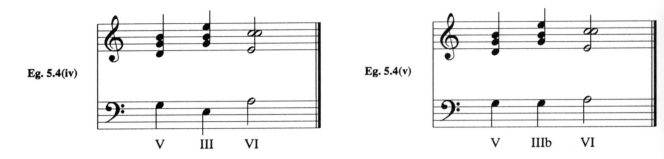

Eg. 5.4(iv)   Eg. 5.4(v)

(ii)   This gives an alternative harmonisation of LN–1 when the LN is a long note:

Eg. 5.4(vi)

e)   When the melody at the end of a phrase moves 3–1 and a final cadence is needed, IIIb—I must be used.

Eg. 5.4(vii)

NB.
The 5th of I has to be omitted.

Otherwise, the notes 3–1 can be harmonised with III—VI.

f)   <u>MINOR KEY</u>

III in the harmonic minor is an augmented chord.

If used in a harmonic minor context, it must be followed by VI.

The augmented note will rise a semitone.

Eg. 5.4(viii)

$$\text{I}\qquad\text{III}\qquad\text{VI}\qquad\text{IIb}\qquad\text{V}$$

g)   IIIb is often used.

h)   III in the descending melodic minor is major, and can be freely used.

Eg. 5.4(ix)

$$\text{VI}\qquad\text{III}\qquad\text{IV}$$

EXERCISE 14 — THE MEDIANT CHORD

5.5   THE LEADING NOTE (LN) CHORD VII

a)   In root position it is a diminished chord and cannot be used. However, in its 1st inversion, it loses its diminished character and is often used.

b)   In the Ia—VIIb—Ib progression, it is a more colourful alternative to the passing $^6_4$ progression.

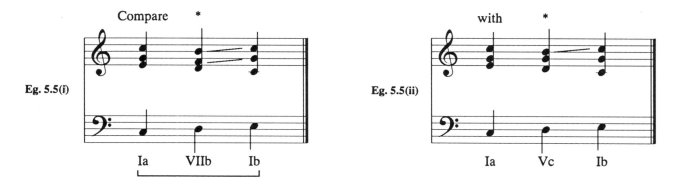

N.B.   In VIIb—Ib, the dim. 5th of VIIb **must** rise, as shown; this avoids doubling the major 3rd of Ib.

c)   Ib—VIIb—I gives a gentle cadential effect, for example when the bass moves 5–4–3–2–1:

d)   The LN itself and the major 3rd of I should not be doubled.

Both the LN and the 5th of the chord should resolve by step.

The bass of VIIb should always be doubled.

EXERCISE 15 — THE LEADING NOTE CHORD

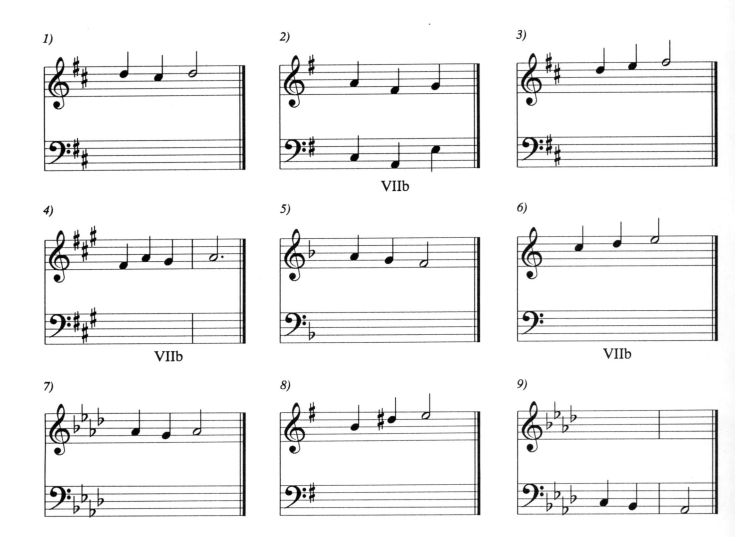

EXERCISE 16 — PRIMARY AND SECONDARY CHORDS

1. Complete the following, using $\frac{5}{3}$, $\frac{6}{3}$ & $\frac{6}{4}$ chords. Use a secondary chord when × is marked.

    NB.   1.   Write 3 notes in the treble stave and 1 in the bass stave.
           2.   Indicate the chords used.

CHAPTER 6

PART WRITING – S.A.T.B.

6.1 It is now time to give attention to the arrangement of chords in the traditional layout:

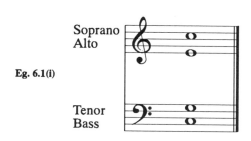

Eg. 6.1(i)

Approximate ranges:

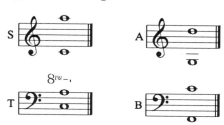

6.2 DOUBLING

General Points

a)   This is the duplication of one of the notes in a triad to form a 4-part chord.

b)   The 5th of a chord can be omitted but not the 3rd:

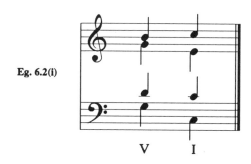

Eg. 6.2(i)

c)   **Root position chords:**

(i)   Major — Double the root.

If this is impossible, double the 5th.

Try to avoid doubling the major 3rd of primary chords.

NB.   The major 3rd of V is the LN and can **not** be doubled.

(61)

(ii)   Minor — Double the root or the 3rd.

        eg.   VI is used mostly in root position, with the 3rd doubled:

Eg. 6.2(ii)

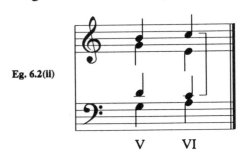

(iii)   Diminished — Except for II, with the root doubled, these chords are not used in root position.

(iv)   Augmented — Double the root.

        eg.   III, which in the minor key is an augmented triad:

Eg. 6.2(iii)

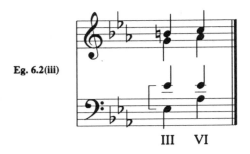

d)   **1st inversion chords:**

(i)   Major — Do not double the 3rd.

(ii)   Minor — Double the bass note, i.e. the minor 3rd of the chord.

Eg. 6.2(iv)

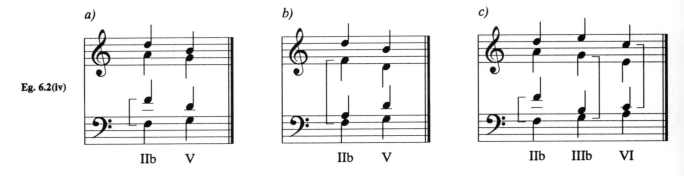

NB.   IIb (with the 3rd doubled) is very commonly used.

(iii)   Diminished

(iv)   Augmented   } Double the bass note.

Eg. 6.2(v)

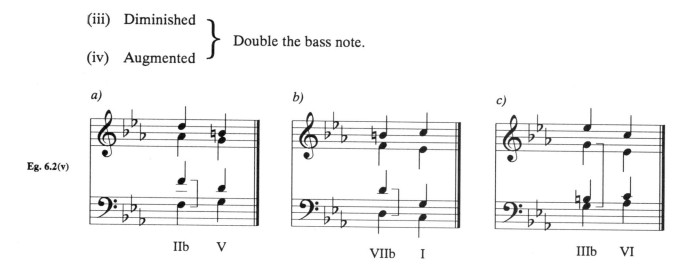

IIb   V   VIIb   I   IIIb   VI

NB.   In the minor key, II and VII are diminished chords and III an augmented one.

e)   **Second inversion chords** (Cadential and Passing $\frac{6}{4}$ s):

(i)   The bass notes of Ic and IVc are doubled.

(ii)   The root of the other chord of the progression is doubled.

Eg. 6.2(vi)

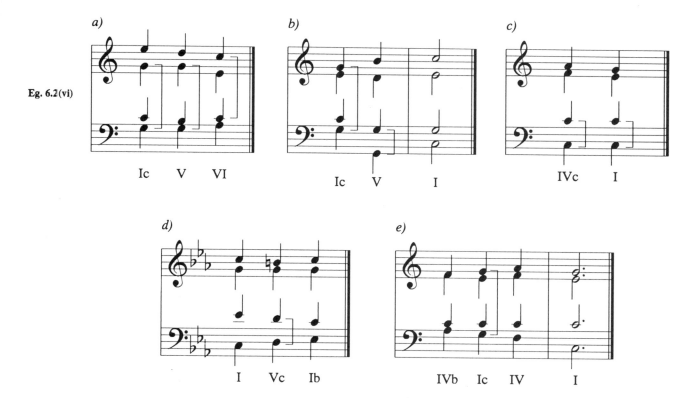

Ic   V   VI   Ic   V   I   IVc   I

I   Vc   Ib   IVb   Ic   IV   I

f) **General rule for doubling:**

When a note of a triad is predetermined in its movement (eg. LN, which must rise to the tonic in V—I), it cannot be doubled; consecutive 8ves would result.

Only the "free" note of a triad may be doubled.

6.3 SPACING

a) Spacing is the arrangement of the notes within a chord.

Eg. 6.3(i)

NB.

The interval between adjacent parts must not exceed an 8ve except between the bottom two parts.

b) **Overlap** occurs when parts cross:

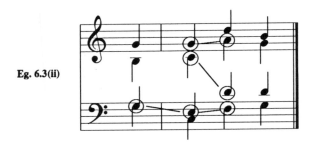

Eg. 6.3(ii)

It is best to avoid this.

6.4 CHORDS IN PROGRESSION

a)   **Movement of individual parts**

This needs care, always. Try to ensure smoothness and avoid awkward intervals:

(i)   When adjacent chords have notes in common, try to keep such notes in the same voice(s):

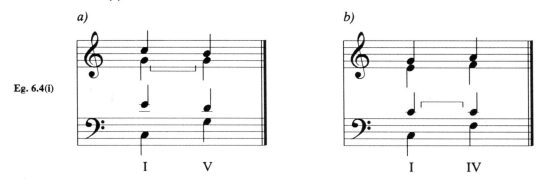

Eg. 6.4(i)

(ii)   The LN must rise to the tonic, whichever voice it is in, when V is followed by I or VI.

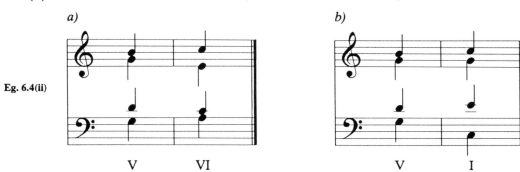

Eg. 6.4(ii)

(iii)   The bass part will often move more boldly than the other voices. This should not be excessive, for the result can be restless. The use of $\frac{6}{3}$ chords will help to give a smoother effect:

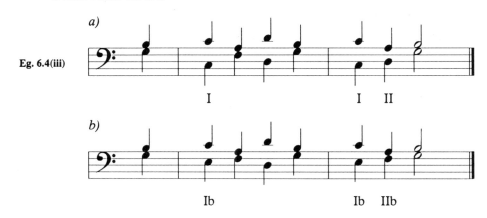

Eg. 6.4(iii)

(iv)   The soprano part needs interest.
       While at first it is wise to observe common notes where possible, the soprano part
       should eventually have melodic interest, helped by a careful mixture of movement
       by step and by leap.

(v)   Augmented rising intervals are not allowed. Inversion of the interval will avoid them:

a)   *b)*

Eg. 6.4(iv)

(vi)   The jump of a diminished interval should be followed by a note which lies within
       the diminished interval, as above.

(vii) **Consecutive** or **parallel** 5ths and 8ves:

       This is the movement of two voices in perfect 5ths and 8ves either in a similar
       direction or in opposite directions:

Eg. 6.4(v)      Eg. 6.4(vi)

It must be avoided.

(viii) **Hidden** (sometimes called **exposed**) 5ths and 8ves:

       This is the result of outer parts moving in the same direction, up or down, on to a
       perfect 5th or 8ve with the top part not moving by step:

Eg. 6.4(vii)   Eg. 6.4(viii)

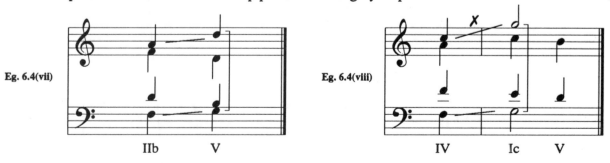

However, if the top part moves by step, the fault is avoided.

(ix)   Movement in opposite directions in the outer voices will avoid hidden 5ths and 8ves, will help to avoid consecutive 5ths and 8ves, and will tend generally to give stronger results than movement in similar directions.

b)   **Doubling in Progressions**

Doubling needs care in certain progressions, to avoid consecutives. It is particularly important with chords which have no common note:

(i)   IV—V

Aim for contrary movement of the outer voices, with the 5th and 8ve of IV moving in opposite direction to the bass:

Eg. 6.4(ix)

IV   V   I

(ii)   IVb—Vb in major keys

Double the 5th of one chord and the root of the other:

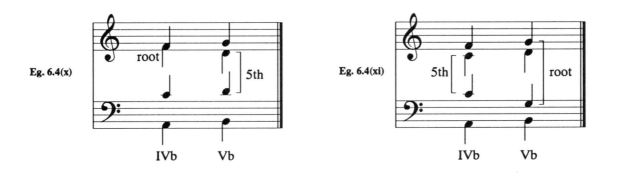

Eg. 6.4(x)   root   5th   Eg. 6.4(xi)   5th   root

IVb   Vb   IVb   Vb

NB.   This progression can not be used in minor keys because of the augmented 2nd which would result in the bass.

(iii)   V—VI

Double the minor 3rd in VI.
Approach or leave the 3rd in opposite directions, so that consecutive 5ths and
8ves are avoided.

Eg. 6.4(xii)

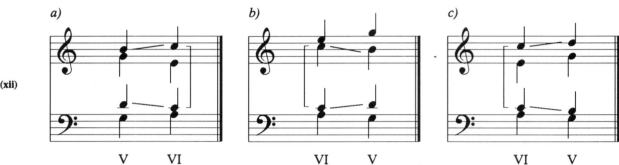

(iv)   II—V and IIb—V

Like IV—V, move the parts in the opposite direction to the bass.

Eg. 6.4(xiii)

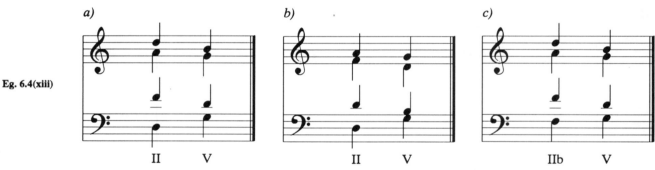

NB.   IIb is best arranged with the root of the chord in the top voice.

c)   When two positions of the same chord are used in succession, the 1st must be on a stronger
beat than the 2nd.

Eg. 6.4(xiv)

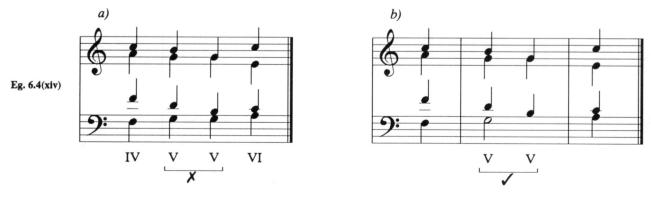

Similarly, a bass note should not be repeated weak–strong.

EXERCISE 17 — PART WRITING AND PROGRESSIONS

Write the following progressions for S.A.T.B. in the specified keys (write in the key signatures).

1. CADENTIAL $^6_4$ $^5_3$

F major    B major    E minor 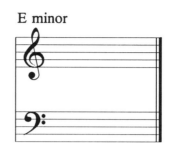   C♯ minor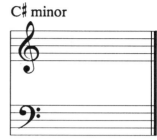

2. PASSING $^6_4$

A minor    D major 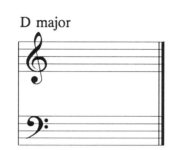   E♭ major    G minor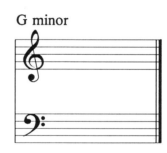

3. PERFECT CADENCE (vary the melody)

E major    F♯ minor    B♭ major    A minor

4. PLAGAL CADENCE (again with melodic variety)

G major    A♭ major 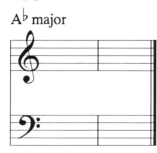   D minor    F minor

5.   IMPERFECT CADENCE (vary the 1st chord in each)

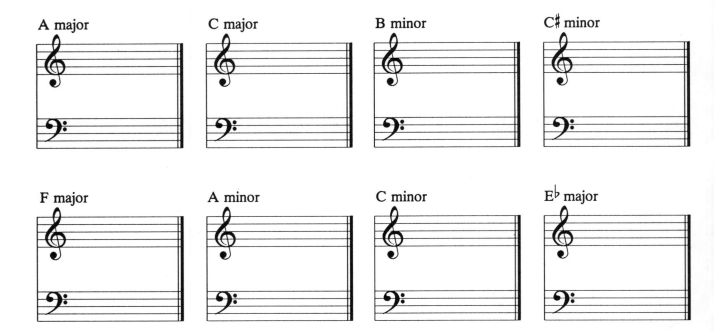

A major   C major   B minor   C# minor

F major   A minor   C minor   E♭ major

6.   INTERRUPTED CADENCE

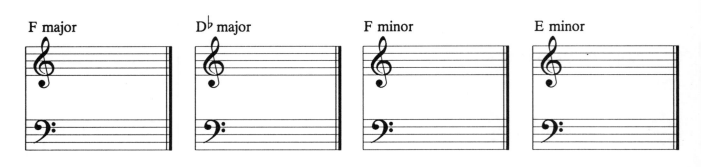

F major   D♭ major   F minor   E minor

7.   IIb—V—I

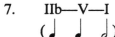
(♩ ♩ ♩)

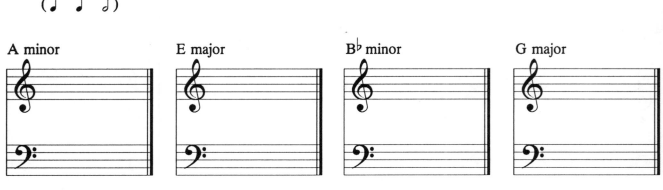

A minor   E major   B♭ minor   G major

8.   IIb—Ic—V—VI

D major   D♭ major   E minor

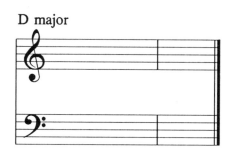
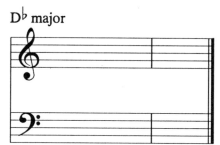
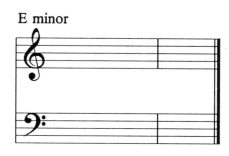

9.   Ib—IIb—V—VI

G major   B♭ major   C minor

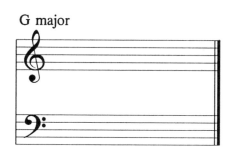
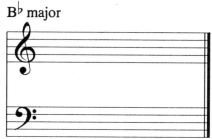
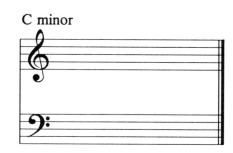

10.   I—VI—IIb—V

D major   G minor   F major

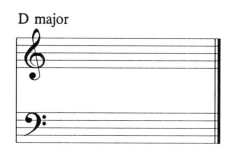
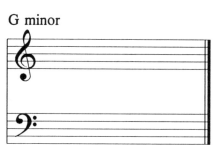
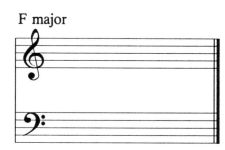

11.   I—IV—Ib—VIIb—I

G major   C minor

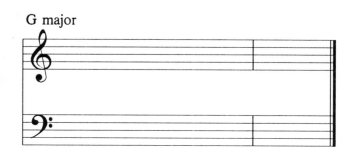
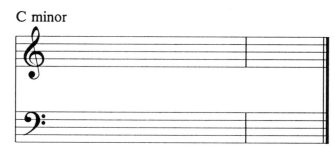

A major

B minor

12.   VI—III—IV—I

B♭ major

F major

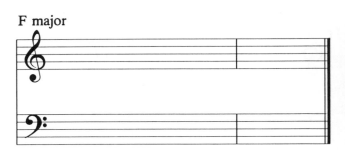

B major

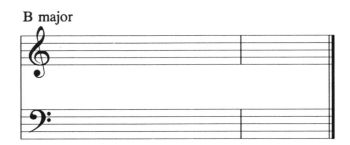

C minor

ROY WILKINSON

Roy Wilkinson, MA., GRSM., ARCM., has been involved in music education for all his professional life. He studied at the Royal College of Music, London, and at Sidney Sussex College, Cambridge. Director of Music first of the City of London School, then of Marlborough College, he is a piano teacher, adjudicator, writer and lecturer, and for many years has been an examiner for the Associated Board of the Royal Schools of Music, for which he has travelled extensively throughout the world.

Other Classical Spectrum Publications
by Roy Wilkinson & Maria Chen:-

ABC of Theory Series	*Grades 6, 7, 8*
ABC of Aural Awareness Series	*Grades 1 – 6*
(In preparation)	*Grades 7, 8*

Published by

CLASSICAL SPECTRUM PTE LTD

7 Pandan Valley

#07-502 Poinciana Tower

Singapore 597631

Tel/Fax: (65) 4693626

Sole Distributors

WORLDWIDE except Singapore, E. & W. Malaysia, Hongkong

Boosey & Hawkes Music Publishers Ltd

The Hyde, Edgware Road

London NW9 6JN, U.K.

Tel: (44) 181-2053861   Fax: (44) 181-2003737

Singapore, E. & W. Malaysia, Hongkong

Rhythm MP Sdn. Bhd.

2060 & 2061, Jalan Persekutuan, Permatang Tinggi Light Industry,

14000 Seberang Perai Tengah,

Penang, Malaysia.

Tel: (60) 4-5873689   Fax: (60) 4-5873691

E-mail: rhythm_mp@mphsb.po.my

Typesetting & typography

Sinfonia Data n Services

Kent Ridge P. O. Box 1042

Singapore 911102

Tel: (65) 7650619   Fax: (65) 7650609

Printed by

Monosetia Sdn. Bhd. (c/o Rhythm Distributors Sdn. Bhd.)